## ADVANCE PRAISE FOR
### *TEACHING WITHOUT TEACHING*

This deeply personal account of a committed teacher serves as a universal tract about the meaning and value of writing and teaching. It defends higher education as essential to human growth rather than a tool for more successful workforce participation. Parker's questions are a powerful method that directly engage the reader. The book is deceptively short but stimulates ongoing thinking. It belongs on the bookshelf of anyone who cares about the future of higher education—and humanity.

—Nora Demleitner, former president of
St. John's College (Annapolis)

Scott Parker provides us not an instruction manual on pedagogy but a vital book of meditations that will keep you coming back to reflect on the purpose of language, the pedagogical ego, and the sacred opportunity of the classroom. In an age of obsessive focus on measurable outcomes, he challenges us to remember—and to grow—the humanity of our students, our teachers.

—Alice Dreger, award-winning educator and writer,
author of *Galileo's Middle Finger*

Teaching means not just asking if students are learning, but what they're learning, how they're learning, and when they're learning. *Teaching without Teaching* provides us a model for reflective teaching practice that shows there is no endpoint to exploring these questions.

—John Warner, author of *More Than Words: How to Think About Writing in the Age of AI*

Scott Parker has written us a gift. Part manifesto, part philosophical meditation, *Teaching without Teaching* reminds us just what an education is for. With wit, humility, and candor, we trace Parker's own pedagogical journey, as he comes to embrace ambiguity and authenticity over performative disagreement and false certitude. This is a book—itself a model of lucid prose—for anyone who is interested in writing and thinking more clearly or simply living in a truer way.

—Thomas Chatterton Williams, author of *Summer of Our Discontent: The Age of Certainty and the Demise of Discourse*

# TEACHING WITHOUT TEACHING

## SCOTT F. PARKER

ONE SUBJECT PRESS

2025

**TEACHING WITHOUT TEACHING**
Scott F. Parker

Editing by Zach Czaia
Cover Image by Tanja Prokop
Text design and typesetting by Andrea Reider

Earlier versions of these essays appeared in *Inside Higher Ed,
The Chronicle of Higher Education*, and *Whale Road Review.*

Published by One Subject Press, 715 Cherokee Avenue,
Saint Paul, MN 55107, www.onesubjectpress.com

ISBN: 978-1-967900-00-8

Printed in the United States of America by Total Printing
Systems

Year 30 29 28 27 26 25

Printing 10 9 8 7 6 5 4 3 2 First

Text printed on 30% post-consumer recycled paper

*For my students*

# CONTENTS

# I.

## TEACHING WITHOUT TEACHING

or

## A PEDAGOGY OF AUTHENTICITY

or

## A MANIFESTO FOR ONE

# WRITING AS BEING

1.  Writing is not a collection of skills. It is not the tricks of the trade. It is not a mastery of craft. It might involve these things, but it is not them.
2.  Writing is a way of life, a way of being.
3.  As with most ways of being, one may be initiated into the writing life. Which is to say it may be learned. Which is to say it may be taught.
4.  How is it learned? *Curiosity, appreciation, admiration, practice, effort, love, dedication.* So many words come rushing to mind, all of them orbiting *wonder.* Only later does *instruction* come also to mind.
5.  How is it taught? By making one's own learning public, by maintaining one's wonder.
6.  When the student is ready, the saying goes, the teacher appears.
7.  If the saying did not end there it would go on to say, And when she appears it will be not as a teacher but as herself. You relate to her as a teacher through your apprenticeship.
8.  Her enthusiasm she shares. Her devotion she models. Her way of being, it becomes contagious. (And if you do not contract the contagion, do not

worry. You may be immune to the writing bug, at least this strain of it.)

9.  I will exaggerate to make the point, but only slightly: Everything I know about writing I know from watching how Debra Gwartney looks her students in the eye.

10.  The student–teacher relationship is one to one and determined by the student.

11.  Writing, like Jesus, is medicine for the sick. You remember all those Sunday School kids sneaking off to roll joints in the bathroom. But you also remember the despairing nighttime souls who found in Christ their only possible salvation. You remember them well. Were you not one of them?

12.  The implications for a university are there to be noticed. If your mission is to educate: 1) no grades; 2) no degrees; 3) open the doors; 4) let the learning begin.

13.  Teaching what you know seems good, better than teaching what you don't know, but maybe not as good as not teaching what you know.

14.  If I remember right, on the first day of his counseling classes, Carl Rogers would sit down and say to his students, "So, what should this class be about?" If I were a better teacher, this would be my pedagogy, too.

15. A teacher must teach what he knows, sure. More profoundly, he must be who he is. And he must teach whomever is there to learn.

16. If you want to get better at writing, practice writing. If you don't, don't. The uselessness of writing is what makes it holy.

17. Case in point: How am I writing this manifesto? The way I scratch an itch. And before I started writing there was no itch there to scratch.

18. The being is in the doing. The doing is in the being. The writing is in the writing. The practice is the practice, says my yoga teacher, a master of teaching without teaching.

## WRITING AS THINKING

1. Writing is a method of thinking, I tell my students.

2. "I write entirely to find out what I'm thinking," says Joan Didion.

3. Why am I writing this essay? Because I want to find out what it has to say.

4. How did I learn to write? No one taught me. I got interested in it. That's all. And then everyone started teaching me. Dave Eggers. Zadie Smith. Henry Alley. Bob Dylan. Emerson. Nietzsche. Didion. Wallace. David Shields. Eula Biss. Cheri

Register. Jude Nutter. Patricia Weaver Francisco. Natalie Goldberg. Basho. Issa. Ikkyū. Dōgen. Lao Tzu. Chuang Tzu. And on and on we could go through a Borgesian library of gifts.

5. If you want to write, you'll figure out how.

6. I started writing the things I needed to write. Case in point: *teaching philosophy as manifesto.*

7. My teaching philosophy, whatever else it may be, must be authentic to my genealogy, must be grounded in who I am. Who is that? I'm finding out as I go, sentence by sentence, influence by influence, class by class.

8. You sign up for a class, you get the teacher you get and not some other teacher. The only thing one teacher has to offer that another assuredly does not is himself.

9. There is one way I have found to avoid feeling like an imposter. Show up and be myself without apology. It sounds like such a low bar.

10. I am what I am. Someone who doesn't want to waste time trying to teach people what they don't want to know. Someone who asks, How do I make them want to know? Someone who answers, By putting them in the company of good writing, the company of good thought, and letting nature run its course.

11.  Not *doing* enough? Determined to push water uphill? Still feel like a fraud up there in front of the class? Feel deeply into the feeling of fraudulence. It can be one form authentic feeling takes.

12.  I am what I am. Someone who feels like he isn't well read. Someone who never "received" an "education." Someone who isn't as smart as many of the people he interacts with. Someone who should be taking the class, not teaching it. I have so much more to learn.

13.  So I am who I am, walking the path I walk, recalling what has brought me to where I am.

14.  As a teacher, I try to apply the methods that I have found most effective as a student, foremost of which is to treat students like capable thinkers in their own right (as John Lysaker and Debra Gwartney did with me). Often, they will naturally rise to meet the expectation. They can frequently be wiser than I or they realize.

15.  Many of my most rewarding teaching moments come after a class is over and a former student writes to thank me for making them think and not making them think what I want them to think.

16.  This is my pedagogy: to establish the possibility for each of us, myself included, to become ourselves.

## WRITING AS CARING

1.  I try to meet my students where they are, person to person.
2.  I try to see in them the human first, the student second.
3.  I invite them to care about writing, trusting that if they care the writing will take care of itself. And I try to hold no grudges when they decline my invitation.
4.  *When the student is ready, the teacher appears* becomes *When the desire appears, the effort follows. How do I do what I want to do?* becomes *How have others done something similar?* Or looked at from the other direction: *I like that* becomes *I want to try that.* In this way, one takes the writer's trajectory.
5.  I find myself thinking back again to how I learned how to write. No, that can't be the right construction. I didn't *simple past* learn to write. I *present perfect* have learned how to write, just as I am *present progressive* learning all the time how to write. It is this ongoingness that draws me to writing, this sense of slow growth toward the chance for still more growth. If writing came more easily, I'd have all the less reason to devote myself to it.

6. I am on the journey I am on. My students are on the journeys they are on. When things go well, we find it advantageous to travel together for the time being.

7. We are sometimes, all of us, in the same room.

# II.

# AGAINST ARGUMENT

For years when I taught freshman composition, I centered the class around argument, the form of writing that I took to be at the heart of academic discourse and intellectual life generally. I assigned my students arguments to read. During class discussions, we tried to understand how these arguments worked and didn't work. We produced counterarguments. Then we produced counterarguments to our counterarguments. And so on.

In this way, I was confident that we could develop the kind of mental agility required to see an issue from multiple perspectives and learn how to put ourselves into the mindset of a person who sincerely holds any given position. If I had a moral agenda, it wasn't often that I admitted it. Instead, I stuck to the terms with which I was comfortable, attempting to explain that such a practice was both rhetorically effective and intellectually admirable. It was rhetorically effective because if we can preempt our interlocutor's criticism, we can lessen its thrust. It was intellectually admirable because it is only by subjecting our views to serious criticism that we find reason to change them such that they are, to our minds, the most defensible views on offer, which, after all, is the point of intellectual life— the pursuit of truth.

Argument, then, becomes a kind of virtuous muscle, one that freshman writing serves to exercise through repetition. Approached this way, the subject of an argument is incidental to the formal moves by which the argument proceeds. It didn't matter in my classes if we were arguing about current events or social policy or historical interpretation as long as we were applying our critical method and practicing the skills of effective argumentation. Amid every argument, I asked: "Are we persuaded? If not, why not?" And from there the argument continued. There was always more to say, another perspective to consider. If in theory this was a means of approaching truth, in practice we never seemed to arrive.

Maybe from the standpoint of the classroom, it's no problem not to achieve consensus. But thinking of the individuals in the room and the number of whom came away from our discussions embracing various versions of epistemological relativism, I began to wonder if I were engaged in a Socratic process that succeeded in undercutting my students' intellectual assumptions but left them adrift in the seas of claim and counterclaim. They got better at taking different perspectives and arguing disinterestedly from various sides on a given issue, but were they losing sight of *their own* perspectives, of which positions they actually held?

Maybe this is a disorienting but necessary phase in intellectual growth during which we must strip down before building back up. But were we building back up? Wouldn't any attempt to build be immediately subjected to the forces of critical examination that would prevent any genuine growth? Wasn't our entire discourse at risk of being ironized into cynicism? Weren't we, in short, well on our way down the road to sophism—or law school?

A few years back, the book *Everything's an Argument* was passed around my department. In it, Andrea A. Lunsford and John J. Ruszkiewicz take the familiar line that every utterance is to some degree rhetorical in the sense that it aims at having some effect on its audience. Call that aim a form of argument (usually informal), and there you have it. But if we understand argument so broadly that everything is an argument, suddenly nothing is an argument. To say that "Hi, how's it going?" is an argument "that your hello deserves a response," as Lunsford and Ruszkiewicz propose, is to define *argument* as only a rhet/comp professor would. It is to have picked up one of Maslow's hammers in grad school and set out in search of nails.

What's so off-putting about this position (one attested to by no less an essayist than Meghan O'Gieblyn in her book *Interior States*) is not that it's pedantic and dorky, but that it's dehumanizing. It treats people as merely self-interested actors making "arguments" to the world in our continuing attempts to effect change for the sake of our personal benefit. But what human, full of feeling, would allow themselves to be so flagrantly reduced? If we were actually to reach this point, we writing teachers might just as well give up the ghost and walk across campus to beg admittance to the economics department.

At its basis, every genuine argument makes the same point: "my way of thinking about things is superior to your way of thinking about things." But don't we have more interesting things to say than "I'm right, and you're wrong"? Don't we want to?

Maybe anyone who believes that everything is an argument deserves to. Maybe, as far as they are concerned, everything is. And maybe those of us who think language is capable of something more are also right. Everything, in other words, can be an argument. But it doesn't have to be. And the question is, which world you'd rather live in.

To think of all those classroom hours arguing for the importance of argument, each one followed by a return to my desk, where argument was largely incidental to my writing life, is to think of myself as I thought of so many of my teachers: adults whose careers depended on their not admitting to themselves that much of what they said was bullshit. From the comfort of my desk, what I knew myself to be engaging with was inquiry, was practice, was the honorable and mysterious pursuit of art. Sometimes I did engage in argument, but afterward I always felt like I needed a shower.

Allow me an example: On the issue of mountain lion conservation, I am a committed advocate. When our state governor pays someone to tree a cougar for him so that he may mosey along at his convenience and shoot it point blank, you can count on me to write a letter to the editor attempting to get my fellow Montanans to see him as selfish, entitled, and a disgrace to the state. But I'd be lying if I said saving mountain lions was my only motivation to write such letters. There's also my wanting to demonstrate my moral and intellectual superiority. *Look at me,* I'm always saying. *Not bad, eh.*

While I stand by the righteousness of my views, I'm deeply aware that operating in this mode does not bring out the best in me. It's a needy and power-hungry side of myself that seeks victory. To that end, I will seek out information and arguments that support the position I am already committed to. I write to win.

Even writing about writing in this mode makes me want to distance myself from my aggression and work toward something gentler in myself. My yoga teacher, Sara Clary, says that yoga is a conversation. The poses ask questions that the body answers. Such a conversation, I recognize, cannot be rushed. And neither can such a conversation be concluded. The conversation of yoga, like all good conversations, is ongoing.

That is the way writing sometimes is, too. When we engage with the process of writing as the goal of writing we are free to explore and express through language, free to proceed by association and intuition, free to accept ourselves as we are, free to trust, free to receive, free period. Instead of writing being a means of affecting change in the world, a means always pointed toward some future end, it can be experienced as something like an end in itself. Approached that way, writing may lead us to some final product or otherwise produce some tangible worldly result, or it may not. And either is beside the point, which is simply to write and be curious about what results.

Argument cuts in another direction. Whereas writing practice is the domain of the curious, argument is the discourse of the insecure. The persuasive writer is necessarily defensive, knowing that his position requires all the support it can muster and that it will never be enough. (Just look at me here, making this argument against argument. What will it take to convince you? What will it take to convince myself?)

Back to the classroom. The reasons to teach argument are obvious. Argument is useful. Argument is the easiest kind of writing to teach. Argument is easy to evaluate and critique.

But the reasons not to teach argument (or not to teach so much of it) are obvious, too. Argument is (too) easy. Argument as such is vacuous. Argument is a small part of what writing can be. Why limit a class unnecessarily?

Sometimes in class I will ask my students to think of the most important things they've changed their minds about and what made them change. I find this a beneficial exercise to conduct on myself as well. When I do, what I find is that rarely have I changed my mind about something I consider important in direct response to an argument. Even in moments when I've acquiesced in the face of an argument I could not effectively rebut, the defeat hasn't really changed my mind as much as allowed me a retreat from which to determine where my argument let me down and how I can improve it for future encounters.

No one, that is, has successfully talked me into or out of my political commitments, my moral concerns, or my religious sympathies. And yet in all those arenas I have had my mind changed, and I consider these changes among the most profound factors in my self-identity.

What, then, has changed my mind? Feelings, first. The "reasons" my politics have shifted now and again always trail my intuitions and my sympathies. And when they shift again, the causes will be the same. In other words, no matter how astute a self-observer I can be, I will always be playing catchup to my mysterious self. If that begs the question of intuitions and sympathies, we can go there. Relationships—whether mediated or, especially, personal—have their way with me. Other people—their sensibilities, their concerns, their humanity—rub off on me. Is this logical? Not strictly. It is, though, as far as I can tell, inescapably human.

I drop my guards when my interlocutors relate to me as a person and not as the beneficiary of some correct position they will impart to me. My mind is changed most, and most lastingly, by those who exhibit no interest in changing it.

But if such experiences change my mind more effectively than argument, what is argument for?

I won't deny the formal beauty of a good argument. There is something intellectually and aesthetically satisfying in seeing someone proceed from sound premises to justified conclusion. Nor will I deny that it is useful in certain conscribed contexts when someone is aiming for dispassionate judgment, often with a forced choice to follow (courtrooms, certain academic spaces, voting booths). But these are narrow and purposeful applications where things can be settled to some reasonable extent. So much of life, though, remains unsettled. And there, in the unsettled, is where we live most of the time.

In a liberal arts seminar I teach, where the focus is less on writing per se than on how to engage academically with diverse material in diverse disciplines, we read Ruth Grant's "The Ethics of Talk." In it, Grant lays out a case for the classroom as a site for dialogue rather than debate. The distinction being that "Unlike debate, a dialogue is a conversation in which different opinions are critically evaluated, distinctions are made, and argument and evidence are put forward with a view to reaching agreement on whatever comes to light as most reasonable—*and* with the expectation that something new and better will come to light."

Often in the classroom, something better does come to light. When things go well, through the indomitable process of democratic engagement, whereby we speak amicably and listen generously, each of our narrow perspectives is subsumed in the discussion itself. As the teacher, I try to step back and listen less to the individuals than to the dialogue as a whole. What I hear are voices unconcerned with being right (or, worse, being seen as being right) and sincere in their expressions of what they understand. Everyone plays their part, and the conversation goes on.

If this is argument—and I think it is—then it is a mode of argument I can get behind. Consider: by examining ideas in the light of reason, we guide ourselves toward clarity and compassion. We don't aspire to convergence or persuasion but to understanding. We learn to take pleasure in the very fact of the range of opinions on offer. We let our own minds be changed as cognitive empathy pulses through our discourse.

As inspiring as this might be to humanities types like me, it is awfully far removed from the standard academic discourse, where argument is understood as a site of victory and defeat. And yet so often we insist on training students to write the very things that no one (ourselves included) would ever like to read. We should not forget when speaking of academic writing that it is nearly bad by definition, considering that *academic* is often used to mean "impractical," "useless," or "inane."

That is how it is, but not how it has to be. As a writing teacher, a middle ground is available to me that neither kowtows to argument nor dismisses it. What I have in mind is a humanistic form of argument, one that isn't preoccupied with staving off criticism but that allows, even seeks, vulnerability on the part of its author. That is the synthesis I aspire to, the one in which the student risks thinking aloud, risks an opinion that might be contentious and that they might not hold in perpetuity. Give me writing that explores. Give me students with the courage to think one thing and then another. Give me a classroom that is a shared space of cultivation.

In fact, and along those same lines, I must admit that I came to this essay with only the vaguest sense of what I intended to write. All I really wanted to do was test out some ideas and see where they would lead. As I have been writing this essay, I have been refining my positions all the while. Troubled by the role of argument in the writing classroom, I have been attempting to discover my attitude toward it. But I trust the writing. I trust that it will lead me to where I want to be, which at least for now is right here: on a note of uncertainty, with nothing resolved, the discussion suspended, awaiting response, ready to be continued.

It is here, in uncertainty, that I aspire to dwell, where argument is a mode of curiosity. As I approach, it is with the voices of George Lakoff and Mark Johnson in my ear, proposing their enchanting alternative to the usual martial metaphors we apply to argument:

"Imagine a culture where an argument is viewed as a dance, the participants are seen as performers, and the goal is to perform in a balanced and aesthetically pleasing way." I never imagined myself a dance teacher, but as I begin another new semester, such is the routine I will be attempting to choreograph.

# III.

# WHAT IS
# EDUCATION FOR?

A s a student, I never had a good answer to a question I was often asked: "What are you going to do with a philosophy degree?" The truth was that thinking about my future wasn't especially interesting to me, at least not interesting in the way philosophy was interesting.

I have been paying for my lack of foresight ever since. In the twenty years following my college graduation, I have earned a grand total of barely any money. Of course, it's hardly philosophy's fault. I know plenty of philosophy majors who have gone on to quite profitable American lives. To the question of what I've "done with a philosophy degree," the answer is this: lived my life, made good decisions and bad decisions, pursued various interests, and accumulated occasional regrets. What that has to do with philosophy is mostly beyond me, except that as I was living my life, I did so with a store of philosophical reference points that I used to coordinate the events of my days and my understanding of them. In other words, it has enriched my inner life—just as it did for me back when I was so busy not thinking about my financial future.

I mentioned regrets. Is studying philosophy one of them? Of course not. However straight the line I could draw from college to "career," wealth, despite the preoccupation with it that I am all the time encouraged to maintain, is not the only value a life may be measured by.

Everyone knows this in theory. And yet, from my student years all the way through to my current position as a university instructor, the only answer to the question of what education is for that I have reliably heard given to students is vocational: Education is preparation for the job market.

Sometimes the promise of a career track is made directly; often it is made indirectly by vague allusions to "transferable skills." Within the humanities, few of the people making this promise, I suspect, believe it with much confidence, but on they go saying it. It is, after all, a thing they've heard before and a thing they still hear, and if academic types are good at anything, it's having an instinct for saying what is in fashion and likely to be well received by their peers. And so common sense emerges.

Students will go on to have careers, of course, but the notion that they will have these careers "because of" their college educations is dubious. (And, by the way, isn't it funny how the academics who make this promise are themselves advertisements against its ultimate fulfillment? Who is taking career advice from a university employee?)

Where has the vocational case gotten us? Common sense is belied by the reality that enrollment has been falling nationally for a decade, and, more and more, those who attend college are not finishing. According to the prevailing logic of higher ed, these data points suggest either that young people no longer care about careers or they are growing increasingly suspicious that college is where they should go to pursue them. Let's assume the latter.

The precipitous decline of enrollment rates in the humanities supports this interpretation: The expected ROI on a humanities degree simply doesn't match that of a STEM degree. And because students are rational economic actors, the rest follows. The cost of college is becoming increasingly prohibitive vis-à-vis future returns.

But wait! We assume students are—and *should be*—rational economic actors? This attitude begs the very questions an education is supposed to ask. What do we value? What should we value? Why? If students come to college (or don't) *because* it is (or isn't) a means of achieving wealth, they do so because they have absorbed the only values they have been offered. They have been failed long before they ever matriculate on our campuses.

Academics don't frame education as a financial matter due to self-hatred. We too have internalized the common denominator of wealth as our sole universal cultural reference point. We speak the language of markets and remuneration because such terms constitute our only shared vocabulary. We speak of these things because it's the only way we can be sure students, prospective students, and their parents will understand us. Worse still, it has become the primary way we understand ourselves.

Thinking of education as a means toward career ends turns our educational institutions into prestigious (or semi-prestigious) credentialing outfits. The attendees (formerly known as students, now more accurately known as "consumers of education") pay for the good they desire. Education is an investment not in themselves as much as in their portfolios. And instead of educators, we come to know ourselves as service providers. The syllabus becomes a contract that students interpret in their favor with the intensity of seasoned lawyers. (If we teach them nothing else, we teach them how to fight for every quantitative good that could possibly be theirs.)

In the classroom we of course ignore the transactional reality of "education." The whole charade of the arrangement depends on it. But when students give their closest readings to syllabi rather than class texts, looking for loopholes they can exploit to the advantage of their grade; when they are unembarrassed to send an email explaining why and how badly they *need* a certain grade; when they fail, again and again, to show up to office hours—then it becomes increasingly difficult to look ourselves in the mirror and maintain eye contact.

What happened to inspiring students to a lifetime of learning and self-reflection? What happened to encouraging them to think critically and creatively about the world they live in and their places in it? What happened to helping them interrogate what it means to be human? Maybe we still are doing these things. But not as much as we could be. Not as much as we hoped to when we started teaching in the first place.

We have only ourselves to blame for this. We ceded the debate about the values of education long ago when we adopted the vocabulary of the marketplace and began "incentivizing" students to obtain "proficiency" within certain "skills sets." We should have known better. We should have resisted the forces seeking to reduce and standardize our students according to quantifiable and easily compared measures. We should have fought harder on behalf of the human being as a multitudinous creature. We should have said that poetry is important not because it might lead by some circuitous route to a career in copywriting, but because it enriches the quality of human life, because it is a means by which we can know and deepen ourselves, because it may infuse life with beauty and meaning. We should have been embarrassed to speak of philosophy as training for law school and unembarrassed to speak of philosophy as Aristotle did—as the activity most suited to human nature. We seek an education when one is available to us *because* it is available to us. It is a luxury to be educated, a privilege if ever there was one, and nothing to be frittered away on the likes of wealth maximization.

This is not to withhold sympathy for those students who look around at the economic landscape and—maybe after pausing to estimate the payments they will have to make on the debt they are accruing—quickly beat a path toward the computer-science office. Given the precarious nature of my finances, I occasionally entertain such fantasies myself. But my final calculation continues to be this: I don't know much about what the future holds. There may be political instability, economic hardship, social unrest, or plague ahead. One thing I am certain of is my eventual death. And it is in that context that I consider my life and define the good. I want to flourish according to values I would endorse from beyond the grave.

Last fall the walkways of my campus were lined with lawn signs reading "TODAY IS A GREAT DAY TO FIND AN INTERNSHIP." The subtext was unmistakable: "Don't fall behind in your career before it begins! There is no time to indulge your whims and your mere interests. The financial clock is ticking! Conform. Comply. Succeed!"

Around the same time, Rose Horowitch reported in *The Atlantic* that arriving college students aren't able to read books because they've never been expected to.

Their teachers have instead taught them how to process "informational passages" with an aim toward efficiency and comprehension of the "main idea." You can almost feel the standardized test taking itself. And you can bet that they haven't been expected to read the former staples of high-school education (*Macbeth, The Great Gatsby, Invisible Man, Song of Solomon,* to name a few from my junior year of high school with Ms. Bidwell), but that they have been expected to prepare themselves for internships. Horowitch reports something that should be apparent to every college professor: "Students today are far more concerned about their job prospects than they were in the past. Every year, they tell Howley [chair of the Literature Humanities program at Columbia University] that, despite enjoying what they learned in Lit Hum, they plan to instead get a degree in something more useful for their career."

This reality is understandable, though lamentable. But this uninspired realism risks being upended by the emergence of AI, which exposes the vacuity of education as vocational training. How do you prepare yourself for a job market that can carry on more efficiently without you? If the goal of education has been to produce workers with the skills necessary to do high-quality work, and automation makes the cost of such human labor prohibitively expensive, what becomes the purpose of education? The coming AI reality should have no special bearing on how we approach education except to clarify its virtues. The education we should pursue in this new context is the education we should have been pursuing all along.

If the point of an education is to think better—and, perhaps, eventually think *well*—then, simple and difficult as that is, education has a lot more in common with music and sports than it does with factory workers producing widgets to take to market. We play piano as we play soccer as we play chess as children simply *play*, because doing so is (or at least can become) its own reward. It is, in a word, *fun*. That these activities often enrich our lives is incidental to our pursuit of them. Our object is engagement, absorption, concentration, delight. Education—*true* education—is no different. The instrumental rewards that attend to it are ancillary to its essence. Some of us may be individuals in pursuit of niche careers. All of us are students of the human condition. This is where we reside: reflecting on the nature of things from as many vantages as can be made available to us.

If we don't produce a forceful articulation of what it is we do and why, we will continue to be subject to that old complaint: "When am I ever going to *use* this?" Instead of making the case that the skills we teach students are transferable across a multitude of career fields, we should be saying something much stronger: The skills we are teaching bypass all career fields and move directly to the core of who we are and what we do. Our area is the human being in the broadest-possible scope.

The only reason to go to college should be that you care about education as such. The intrinsic good of education is what matters, not the extrinsic rewards. The failure to make this distinction—or, worse, to invert it—lies at the heart of what ails us.

# Acknowledgments

Thank you to Mindy Misener, whose inspiration and encouragement were the starting points for what became this small book.

Thank you to Zach Czaia, publisher of One Subject Press, who read these essays in magazine form and proposed collecting them as a book. Zach, your dedication to publishing reminds me what I love about our literary world.

Thank you to the editors who published these essays in their original versions: Katie Manning, Sarah Bray, and David Wescott. And thank you to Alice Dreger, whose professional support over the past year has been invaluable.

I have been fortunate to learn from many wonderful teachers. Thank you to all of them, especially John Lysaker, Debra Gwartney, and Sara Clary, who remain the primary models I aspire to in the classroom. And thank you to my colleagues and students, with whom I continue to develop my thinking about teaching.

# About the Author

S cott F. Parker is an assistant teaching professor at Montana State University. His writing about pedagogy has appeared in *The Chronicle of Higher Education, Inside Higher Ed, Inquisitive,* and *Assay: A Journal of Nonfiction Studies,* among other publications.

## THE ONE SUBJECT PRESS
## TEACHER/WRITER SERIES

The Teacher / Writer series centers the voices of writers who teach in the humanities, whether to students in the fourth, tenth, or twenty-second grade. It challenges the prescriptive and standardized educational status quo, and fires the imaginations of those hungry for greater depth as both teachers and as writers.

### OTHER TITLES IN THE SERIES